ABUNDANT TRUTH INTERNATIONAL MINISTRIES

Logos Apologetics Series

The Doctrine of Spiritual Warfare

Understanding the Enemy of the Christian

Roderick Levi Evans

Published by Abundant Truth Publishing
P.O. Box 126 * Camden, NC 27921
Phone: 1-877-841-7209 * Fax: 1-877-841-7209
Web: www.abundantpublishing.net
Email: abundantpublishing@gmail.com

Front & Back Cover Designs by Abundant Truth Publishing
Image by Fran Soto from Pixabay

> Abundant Truth Publishing is a ministry of Abundant Truth International Ministries. The primary mission of ATI Ministries is to equip the Body of Christ with tools necessary to defend and contend for the truth of the Christian faith. Jesus Christ came to bear witness of the truth and ATI Ministries is a modern-day extension of His commission (John 18:37).

The Doctrine of Spiritual Warfare: Understanding *the Enemy of the Christian*
©2009 Abundant Truth Publishing
All Rights Reserved

ISBN: 978-1-60141-015-3

No portion of this material may be reproduced, stored in a retrieval system, or transmitted in any form or by any means electronic, mechanical photocopy, recording, or any other except for brief quotations in printed reviews and proper work citation, without the permission of the Publisher.

Contents

Introduction

Chapter 1 – The Devil   1

The Beginning   5

The Blunder   9

The Banishment   15

Chapter 2 – The Devices   27

Life   32

Lies   40

Lust   51

Contents (cont.)

Chapter 3 – The Defeat   **71**

The Armor of God   76

Prayer in the Spirit   84

Praise   86

Bibliography   **93**

Introduction

In his first epistle, Peter admonished Christians to be ready to give unbelievers the reason for their hope in Jesus Christ. In order to do so, they would have to be able to articulate and then defend their faith. The defense that they give would have to be reasonable and sustainable. This was an early call for Christians to be defenders or apologists of the Christian faith.

This commission continues to the present-day Christian. The Logos Apologetics Series is developed as a resource for Christians who want to understand apologetics and the apologetic discipline presently.

In this issue

The devil is real. His number one deception is to cause mankind not to believe in his existence. The Bible tells us otherwise. As believers, we must understand that we have an adversary, and we must engage in spiritual warfare.

Because God is love, debates have been ongoing as to how He could create such an evil being who wreaked havoc on the world. God created Lucifer in all righteousness. But he chose to become corrupt. In this issue, we will provide an introduction to spiritual warfare. It is our hope that Christians will discover who the adversary is and how to overcome him.

-Chapter 1-

The Devil

The Doctrine of Spiritual Warfare | 2

Logos Apologetics Series

The devil is real. His number one deception is to camouflage his existence. The Bible clearly depicts the devil as real and influential being. As believers, we must understand that we have an adversary.

God can only operate in love, for He is love. This is a perplexing situation to some, that a loving God could have such a being. Remember. God created Lucifer in righteousness, but *he* chose to become corrupt. If we are to overcome the enemy, we must understand him.

Anyone in the military will tell you that the best weapon against an enemy is knowledge, not just force. By knowing their enemy, they can fully prepare themselves against their opponent's strength and exploit their weaknesses.

Before examining ways to overcome the devil, we must understand who he is. We will look at His beginning, blunder, and banishment.

The Beginning

The devil's God-given name at his creation was Lucifer. It means "shining star or son of the morning." God created him as one of His archangels. The book of Ezekiel describes the beauty and honor bestowed upon Lucifer.

> *"Son of man, take up a lament concerning the king of Tyre and*

say to him: 'This is what the Sovereign LORD says: "'You were the seal of perfection, full of wisdom and perfect in beauty. You were in Eden, the garden of God; every precious stone adorned you: carnelian, chrysolite and emerald, topaz, onyx and jasper, lapis lazuli, turquoise and beryl. Your settings and mountings were made of gold; on the day you were created they were prepared. You were anointed as a guardian cherub, for so I ordained you. You were on the holy mount of God; you walked among the fiery stones. You were blameless in your ways from the day you were created... (Ezekiel 28:12-15a)

God made Lucifer perfect. He was anointed to stand by God and walk around the throne of God. He was a guardian cherub around the throne.

He was full of wisdom and the perfection of beauty. He was one of God's chief angels and creation. No other angels in the scriptures are given such an awesome description, not even Michael or Gabriel.

God's anointing rested upon Lucifer and God ordained it so. Lucifer was also present at creation for the text says that he was in Eden, not as a serpent, but as the anointed cherub of God.

When we consider all that God had bestowed upon him, it is hard to believe that this is the one whom we now call our adversary. What led to his fall? He stumbled because of his form.

What caused the perfect, beautiful, and wise angel to become a fool? What led to his disaster and ruin? How did he go from a wonder to a blunder?

The Blunder

Lucifer had it all. He was perfect in

all of his ways, but he fell. Further reading of Ezekiel gives us insight into what caused his fall.

> *You were blameless in your ways from the day you were created till wickedness was found in you. Through your widespread trade you were filled with violence, and you sinned. So I drove you in disgrace from the mount of God, and I expelled you, guardian cherub, from among the fiery*

stones. Your heart became proud on account of your beauty, and you corrupted your wisdom because of your splendor... Ezekiel 25:15-17a)

Lucifer fell because of pride. He became puffed up because of his beauty. He became infatuated with himself and he forgot that he was only a creation. This is why Ezekiel said his wisdom was corrupted.

How art thou fallen from heaven,

O Lucifer, son of the morning! how art thou cut down to the ground, which didst weaken the nations! For thou hast said in thine heart, I will ascend into heaven, I will exalt my throne above the stars of God: I will sit also upon the mount of the congregation, in the sides of the north: I will ascend above the heights of the clouds; I will be like the most High. (Isaiah `4:12-14)

Lucifer's plan was to take over. He had a list of things that he would do. He actually accomplished the first two. First, he was already present in heaven ("I will ascend into heaven").

Second, when he stated that he would exalt his throne above the stars of would, he meant that he would exercise authority over the angels (stars) of God. He succeeded only in part because not all the angels shared in his delusion.

Lucifer allowed his beauty, perfection, and wisdom to cloud his judgment. He thought that he could overthrow God. This was his calamity or ruin. He deceived himself. This should serve as a warning to believers today to be aware of pride.

God has gifted many of us to be in His service. We must not allow the things that God has blessed us with to blind and corrupt us. Else, we will find ourselves walking in the way of Lucifer.

Now that we have looked at his beginning and blunder, let us now look at his impending banishment in the bottomless pit.

The Banishment

The banishment and tortuous end of Lucifer will not come until the Day of Judgement. God has already exacted punishment upon him in part.

Michael, the archangel, cast Lucifer and his followers out of heaven after their rebellion against God.

It is believed that the "third of the stars in heaven" that the rail of the red dragon cast down to the earth reveals that a third of the angels in heaven followed him (see Revelation 12).

After being cast out of heaven, his name was changed from Lucifer (shining star) to Satan, which means *adversary*, and also by interpretation, *snake*. He is also contemporarily known as the devil, which means *wicked one*.

He had dominion in heaven as a

guardian cherub. He had authority over some of the angels because he was the "the seal of perfection and beauty." Now, he is referred to as the prince of the power of the air (Ephesians 2:2).

He went from representing the beauty and presence of God to becoming the embodiment of all that is evil. He now works to bring shame to God and His creation, in direct contrast to his former position which worked to honor and glorify the Father in the beginning.

Though his destruction and end has not yet been realized, it will come. He *will* be thrown into the bottomless pit, first. He will subsequently be released and then cast into the lake of fire. He will be tormented for all eternity.

Why?

First, He rebelled against God in the beginning. And second, because of his mission to seduce mankind into sin. When this occurs, the conclusion to Lucifer's story will be complete.

Since we are made in God's likeness and image, he hates us just as much as he hates God. He has the singular mission for mankind – seek and destroy. Our enemy is on his job daily. Because of this, the believer must pray continually and be watchful.

Jesus told the disciples to watch and pray. If they did not watch and pray, they would fall into temptation or into the hands of the evil one (Matthew 26:41). Satan and his fallen angels are at work continually to destroy and deceive me.

In the book of Job, we discover what the enemy does daily. God asks the devil when he had been. His reply should cause us to be sober.

*And the L*ORD *said unto Satan, Whence comest thou? Then Satan answered the L*ORD, *and said,*

From going to and fro in the earth, and from walking up and down in it. (Job 1:7)

Our adversary and the fallen angels are constantly roaming the earth, searching for someone to devour. Why? They are in battle with God over the souls of men.

The enemy will be judged in the last days; therefore, he wants to take as many of us as he can with him to the judgment.

The Christian has to be alert at all times. In addition, the Christian should not be afraid of this spiritual battle. Fear will only paralyze the believer when it is time for spiritual warfare.

God has given us power over the works of the enemy (Luke 10:19). The very reason Jesus came into the world was to destroy the works of the devil (John 3:8). In addition, we find numerous scriptures that confirm and reaffirm the believer's authority over Satan.

Notes:

- Chapter 2 -

The Devices

Logos Apologetics Series

Through the Spirit of God, we are not ignorant of Satan's tactics and schemes (II Corinthians 3:11).

Though the Word is given to us as a weapon against the enemy, many are still defeated by his demonic tactics. We are defeated when we walk in ignorance. We must walk in wisdom.

See then that you walk circumspectly, not as fools but as wise, redeeming the time, because the days are evil. (Ephesians 5:6 KJV)

Walk in Wisdom - See then that you walk circumspectly, not as fools but as wise, redeeming the time, because the days are evil. (Ephesians 5:15-16 AMP)

The reason we must walk in the wisdom and light of God is because the present days are evil. If we do not do this, we will be unwise in our decisions. We will become vulnerable to the schemes of the enemy. We must consistently be alert and aware of demonic activity.

We cannot combat the ploys of the enemy if we do not know what they are. He uses three main tactics/schemes against believers. If we were to examine our personal walks with God, we would find that the enemy has fought us often and we did not realize it. The three main tactics used by the adversary are **_Life, Lust,_** and **_Lies._**

Life *(distractions)*

The devil uses life's problems and occurrences as distractions. As believers, we must not fall into this trap. We cannot become focused on life's situation and lose control over worldly things.

We cannot allow our families and friend to distract us from God. We cannot even allow church work or service to be our singular focus.

The things we do for Christ cannot become more important than our relationship with Him. If this happens, we will fall into the hands of the enemy. We read in the gospels of how Martha worked in the kitchen when Jesus came and of how Mary sat at his feet.

Now it came to pass, as they went, that he entered into a certain village: and a certain woman named Martha received him into her house. And she had a sister called Mary, which also sat at Jesus' feet, and heard his word. But Martha was cumbered about much serving, and came to him, and said, LORD, dost thou not care that my sister hath left me to serve alone? bid her therefore that she help me. And Jesus answered and said unto her, Martha, Martha, thou art careful and troubled about many things: But one thing is needful: and Mary hath chosen that good part, which shall not be taken away from her. (Luke 10:38- 42)

Martha thought she was doing the right thing, but Jesus corrected her. She was so **distracted** trying to serve the Lord, that she was neglecting fellowship with Him. We must learn from Jesus' words. We, oftentimes, become distracted with many of life's concerns and problems.

Moreover, we can be overly concerned with trying to serve the Lord that we miss the blessings of fellowship with Him. In this state, we will be vulnerable to an attack of the enemy.

Distractions in life will cause us to be frustrated like Martha. She could not appreciate and enjoy the presence of Jesus in her home because of them. As believers, we sometimes do not enjoy our salvation because we are too busy with concerns. Martha responded in the wrong spirit due to her frustration.

If we are not careful, our distractions from life will cause undue irritation and frustration. Moreover, frustration will cause us to respond negatively to life and to Christ. Martha rebuked Christ and complained about her sister not helping her. We have to guard against this mindset, which will result in placing blame upon God for our frustration.

If we become subject to this mindset, we become crippled and unable to progress in our relationship with Christ. The enemy's plan would prove successful.

Therefore, we must not allow distractions in life to make us vulnerable to the enemy's attack, resulting in spiritual bondage. We must submit all our cares (distractions) to Christ, as instructed in the scriptures, Jesus said,

Come unto me, all ye that labour and are heavy laden, and I will give you rest. Take my yoke upon you, and learn of me; for I am meek and lowly in heart: and ye shall find rest unto your souls. For my yoke is easy, and my burden is light. (Matthew 11:28-30)

If we allow the Word of God to govern our lives and peace of God to guard our hearts, the enemy will not be able to use distractions to keep us from walking in victory. Let us keep our thoughts and minds focused on the Lord.

Lies

One of the most powerful tactics of the enemy is lies, which breeds deception. Throughout the scriptures, we find examples of men and women falling into this trap.

Eve was lied to in the Garden. Subsequently, she was deceived into going after the forbidden fruit. She ate of it and gave some to her husband.

If we are not alert, we will believe the lies of the devil and adhere to false teachings. In numerous scriptures, Jesus warned His disciples against being deceived. He warned them of false prophets and teachers that would emerge.

Paul warned believes not to be carried away with fables and warped teachings. There is an abundance of scriptural warnings for us no to be on guard. As we proceed, we will look at eh cause of deception and how to avoid the lies of the adversary. His main vehicle for lies is through the deceptions of false teachings.

As soon as we hear the word "deception," we immediately envision cults, erroneous teachings and teachers, and false prophets.

Therefore, many Christians believe they are invulnerable to deception.

They do not understand that deception (through lies) can occur in subtle ways.

For instance, when we do not believe in all the promises of God which are outlined in the scriptures, we are deceived. By not knowing and trusting in the Word, the Christian will settle for all that the enemy will being into their lives.

Along with reading the scriptures, a knowledge and belief in the power of God is necessary. Oftentimes, we study the scriptures, but do not believe that God will perform and intervene in our lives presently, and He did in the biblical accounts. This is deception, birthed out of the lie that God no longer works as He did in day of old.

We must not only hold to the truth of the scriptures, but also believe that the God the scriptures is willing to manifest His power in our lives. If this is not our mindset, the enemy will being us into bondage. Our walk with God will seem futile and lifeless.

> *Jesus replied, "Are you not in error because you do not know the Scriptures or the power of God? (Mark 12:24)*

Jesus gave two reasons as to why one is deceived (believes the lies of the devil). These two reasons apply to us today. The first was ignorance of the scriptures, and the second was ignorance of the power of God.

When the believer does not have a sound knowledge and understanding of the scriptures or of God's continual power, the enemy will bring deception through lies.

We stated earlier that the devil is now referred to as "the prince of the power of the air." This tells us that his tactics resemble the air. We that air cannot be seen, but its influence can be seen all around.

Looking at objects and how they

move helps us to determine wind (air) direction. Sometimes air van be hot or cold, and it can be thick or thin.

We must understand that even though we cannot see the "prince," he is at work for we need only to look at his effects.

His influence is seen in television, heard on live radio, and even felt and seen in the Church. We are wanted to be alert. He has released a host of evil spirits to deceive us.

Now the Spirit speaketh expressly, that in the latter times some shall depart from the faith, giving heed to seducing spirits, and doctrines of devils. (I Timothy 4:1)

It is in these tines that believers have to be careful not fall away from the Church and the faith. Deceitful spirits have been sent to take us away from the truth. Paul states that believers will pay attention (give heed) to doctrines of demons (devils).

We know that a doctrine is a teaching. Demons have been taught of the devil and will try to put their teachings into the hearts men.

We must be careful not to be carried away with demonic doctrine and those who them. Jesus stated,

> *For there shall arise false Christs, and false prophets, and shall shew great signs and wonders; insomuch that, if it were possible,*

they shall deceive the very elect. (Matthew 24:24)

The Word brings personal stability and spiritual clarity, while the power of God brings spiritual life and vitality. Without both of thee, the enemy will keep us blinded.

We will become vulnerable to false teachings. We will not be able to live in or by faith. Our relationship with God will become stagnant and lifeless.

In this state, we will believe every lie that the enemy will being to mind (about God and ourselves). In order to overcome deception, we must draw night to God through the Word and trust that His power will operate in our lives.

Lust

Above life and lies, there is only one tool that the enemy uses most frequently. He uses the lusts present in our flesh to overcome us. He uses our desires and weaknesses against us.

We know that the enemy does not make us sin, but he will exploit our inward compulsion. One of the most celebrated parables is that of the farmer that went out to sow seed (Matthew 13:1-9, 18-23).

Within this parable, we can see how the enemy exploits our desires and weaknesses, using them to attack us. The parable details for us where a seed may land when thrown by a farmer: *by the wayside, upon stony places, among thorns,* and *upon good ground.* Jesus stated that all these places represented those who heard the Word.

Of these four mentioned, the first three areas might also indicate specific areas in a believer's life that the enemy will exploit in order to dominate him.

Some Seeds Fell By The Wayside...

The first illustration Jesus used to

describe where some seeds fell was by the wayside.

And when he sowed, some seeds fell by the wayside, and the fowls of the air came and devoured them up. (Matthew 13:4 KJV)

The consequence of falling by the wayside was that the birds of the air came down and devoured them. Jesus said this referred to those who received the Word, but at some point, the enemy came and snatched it away from them (Matthew 13:18).

Let us consider how this illustrates an attack of the enemy.

The wayside can also represent an unguarded area in our lives for which we have not built up a defense. This, in turn, leaves an opening for an attack of the enemy.

In the parable, the only reason the birds could get to the seeds is that they were out in the open without protection.

We find many believers have certain desires that constantly entrap them. In addition, they have weaknesses for which they have no power to resist. They live in defeat, dominated by desire.

Many are in despair of ever gaining the victory. Even though they pray and hear sermons, they do not find deliverance. For when they hear the sermons, the enemy comes immediately and snatches the Word that they heard.

How does the enemy snatch the Word from the believer? He accomplishes it through fear, doubt, and unbelief. With these tools, the enemy paralyzes the believer. He, inevitably, gives in to his desire and does not resist. This leads to the enemy stealing the Word.

Some Fell Upon Rocky Places...

The second illustration Jesus

used was that some seeds fell upon stony places, without much soil.

And others fell upon the rocky places, where they did not have much soil; and immediately they sprang up, because they had no depth of soil. But when the sun had risen, they were scorched; and because they had no root, they withered away. (Matthew 13:5-6)

The seeds that fell on rocks sprouted quickly because they had no root. Therefore, when the sun came up, they were burned and were dried up.

Jesus said that this referred to those who received the Word with joy but had no foundation. Subsequently, when persecution and tribulation arose, they became overwhelmed and gave up (Matthew 13:31).

A closer examination of these verses shows us that these "rocky places" could also represent those areas in the believer's life where there is a constant battle, making them targets for the enemy. Since there is a struggle, the believer is always looking for help and an answer.

Therefore, when they hear the Word preached, they quickly say that they are delivered or set free. They deceive themselves because they do not take the time to apply the Word to their weak areas.

They do not allow the Word to take root in their hearts. Therefore, when the desire or temptation returns, they cannot handle it and give up. The Word they heard did not have much soil to grow in.

When we claim deliverance prematurely, we set ourselves up for defeat. We will become utterly discouraged and disappointed because we thought we were free when we were not.

The enemy will use this to keep us in bondage and to cause us to lose hope of being delivered. We must not be like those in the parable.

We must allow the Word to settle in us and grow before we claim complete deliverance.

And Some Fell Among Thorns...

The third illustration that Jesus used was that some seeds fell among the thorns.

And others fell among the thorns,

and the thorns came up and choked them out. (Matthew 13:7)

The consequence of these landing among thorns was that the thorns choked them. Jesus said that this referred to those who received the Word, but the cares of the world consume him, making him unfruitful (Matthew 31:22).

Let us consider the above in this manner: the thorns may represent known areas of sin and compromise in the believer's life. We understand that the seeds and thorns were in the same ground. They each need soil to grow.

Nevertheless, in Jesus' parable, the thorns prevailed. This is indicative of the believer who hears the Word consistently but chooses not to apply the Word to his life. The enemy deceives him into thinking that it is O.K. and God understands.

This believer fought for deliverance and victory in the

beginning. However, when he saw that God did not judge him harshly and was patient with him, he decided not to try anymore.

These types of believers feel that since God still blesses them and is with them, then their sin cannot be all that bad. They manipulate the concept that God loves us just as we are.

They do not understand that God will love us the way that we are until we become who we are supposed to be in

Him. Thus, they attend Church and fellowship with believers. They will even grow in the knowledge of God, but their areas of sin will also grow and eventually dominate them.

Ultimately, their desires and the cares of this life control them, making them unfruitful in the kingdom of God. These are believers who hear the Word, but will not change. In this case, there is no conflict with the enemy because they are his to manipulate.

We have seen that the enemy only has three main tactics: life, lies, and lust. His most successful tactic is man's sinful desires. It is what he uses most to keep us from living a victorious Christian life. The enemy keeps the believer in bondage by exploiting his desires and weaknesses.

If he keeps us wrestling with our flesh, we will never overcome. However, once the tools of the enemy are discovered, we need to know what to do. If someone asked you right now about the areas where you are having trouble, you could give them an answer immediately.

However, knowing the problem without a solution is useless and frustrating. We will now look at ways to overcome the enemy and his tactics. Only then can we live in victory.

Notes:

-Chapter 3-

The Defeat

Understanding the devil and his devices is not enough, except the Christian knows how to respond to him. The Word of God gives us the necessary weapons and armor needed to defeat the adversary. Paul gives us the primary list of weapons available to us in Ephesians 6.

> *Put on the whole armour of God, that ye may be able to stand against the wiles of the devil. For we wrestle not against flesh and*

blood, but against principalities, against powers, against the rulers of the darkness of this world, against spiritual wickedness in high places. Wherefore take unto you the whole armour of God, that ye may be able to withstand in the evil day, and having done all, to stand. Stand therefore, having your loins girt about with truth, and having on the breastplate of righteousness; And your feet shod with the preparation of the gospel of peace; Above all, taking the shield of faith, wherewith ye shall be able to quench all the fiery darts of the wicked. And take the helmet of salvation, and the sword of the Spirit, which is the word of God. (Ephesians 6:11-17)

If we learn to adorn ourselves with spiritual armor provided, success will be ours.

The Armor of God

Possessing weapons and armor without understanding them is useless. We shall now examine the armor given to Christians for victory over the devil.

The Sword of the Spirit

All of the pieces of the armor listed, except the sword of the Spirit, are forms of defense. Although they can protect, they do not make effective weapons. Moreover, the only offensive weapon given to us is our present focus, the sword of the Spirit; that is, the word of God.

When Jesus was tested by the devil, He used the word to combat him. We must also use the Word. We must not only quote the scriptures, but also *believe* in them.

We must trust them and be dedicated to the study and application of them in everyday life. If we do not do this, we will be defeated. We must employ the Word of God in spiritual warfare.

The Word in action penetrates through all the devices of the enemy. In order for the Word to do this, the believer must diligently study and skillfully apply the Word through faith. Victory is assured, when the word of God is active in the believer's daily life.

The Belt of Truth (loins girt with truth)

We need every part of the armor if we are going to stand against the enemy. The belt of truth is absolutely essential. It helps to hold all of the other pieces of the armor together.

Because Jesus is truth, we can trust in everything that He has said or promised. In addition, we need to be people who hold to the truth without wavering.

The Breastplate of Righteousness

The breastplate of righteousness is also crucial. It denotes our identification with the righteousness of

Christ. Though we were sinners and He righteous, He became sin for us and His righteousness was credited to us through faith in Him. The breastplate protects our heart from guilt and shame and it fortifies an inward defense that our hearts will not be defiled with wicked imaginations resulting in sinful activities.

Feet Shod (Sandaled) with the Preparation of the Gospel of Peace

Our feet must be sandaled with

the preparation of the gospel of peace. Tis means that we ought to stand in readiness to take and share the gospel with us everywhere and be led by peace.

The Shield of Faith

The shield of faith is need for your protection. Without faith, the rest of the armor will not hold up under enduring spiritual attacks. Our faith in God is what keeps us through trials, tests, and other attacks of the enemy.

Many believe that faith is the most power weapon against the enemy. However, faith cannot be gained except through the Word.

So, faith comes by hearing, and hearing by the Word of God. (Romans 10:17)

Faith is most important in our walk with God, but faith in the Word is crucial in spiritual warfare It (the Word) alone is the ultimate weapon against eh enemy. When Jesus was confronted by the devil, He did not say, "I have faith," but He declared, "It is written."

Through the Word, we know what power and authority we have, and how to exercise it. If we know, understand, and apply the Word (through and by faith), we will defeat the enemy.

The Helmet of Salvation

The helmet of salvation is need so that the believer will maintain confidence in his or her salvation. The helmet is used as a shield against the lies and tactics that the enemy brings to the mind.

Prayer in the Spirit

Alongside the Word, prayer is essential in spiritual warfare. Prayer increases the efficacy of the power of the Word in our lives. Jesus prayed and fasted for forty days and nights, and then rose up used the Word to defeat the enemy.

Alongside with possessing the

armor, Paul exhorts the Ephesians to pray and intercede. Paul understood that prayer is what gives the armor its effectiveness and strength. Without prayer, the armor is less effective.

Praying always with all prayer and supplication in the Spirit, and watching thereunto with all perseverance and supplication for all saints. (Ephesians 6:18)

Paul states that we must not only pray, but also pray *in* the Spirit. Only then will our warfare against the enemy be most effective.

Primary is the Word of God, and second is prayer. Both are effective offenses against eh devil Prayer alongside with Word forms a most powerful two-fold weapon in the believer's arsenal.

Praise

We have another weapon that can be used at any time. You do not need a complete understanding of the Bible or make lofty prayers. It is the weapon of praise. Both Old and New Testaments attest to the fact that God seeks our praise. In addition, we learn that is our responsibility to give Him praise.

God does not *need* our praise for He has angels that fly before the throne day and night giving Him honor and glory. When we praise God, it is a sign of our appreciation for all that He has done. In addition, praise can be an awesome force against the enemy.

When facing overwhelming situations, we must remember that praise thoughts the heart of God. It is sweet smelling odor in His nostrils.

The scriptures say that God *inhabits the praises* of His chosen people Israel, and we now are His chosen people through Christ.

But thou art holy, O thou that inhabitest the praises of Israel. (Psalm 22:3)

As we praise, God's presence and power manifests. When this occurs, the forces of darkness must flee. If we learn to praise, we will allow God to fight for us. We must remember that our praise can be an instrument of destruction against all the works and tactics of the enemy.

Our battle against the devil is rea and sometimes it gets hard. Nevertheless, if we endure the hard times, we will overcome. We must not faith, for at an appointed time, we will reap the benefits of our labor in Christ.

And let us not be weary, in well doing, for in due season we shall reap, if we faint not. (Galatians 6:9)

In order for us to defeat the enemy, we must use the spiritual resources given to us by God through Christ.

Notes:

Bibliography

Lockman Foundation. Comparative Study Bible. Zondervan Publishing House. Grand Rapids, MI, c1984

Smith, William. Smith's Bible Dictionary. Holman Bible Publishers. Nashville, TN. c1994

The Bible Library. The Bible Library CD Rom Disc. Ellis Enterprises Incorporated, (c) 1988 – 2000. 4205 McAuley Blvd., Suite 385,

Oklahoma City, OK 73120. All Rights Reserved.

Notes:

Logos Apologetics Series

www.ingramcontent.com/pod-product-compliance
Lightning Source LLC
Chambersburg PA
CBHW050343010526
44119CB00049B/669